DISCARD

The HOMEMAKERS

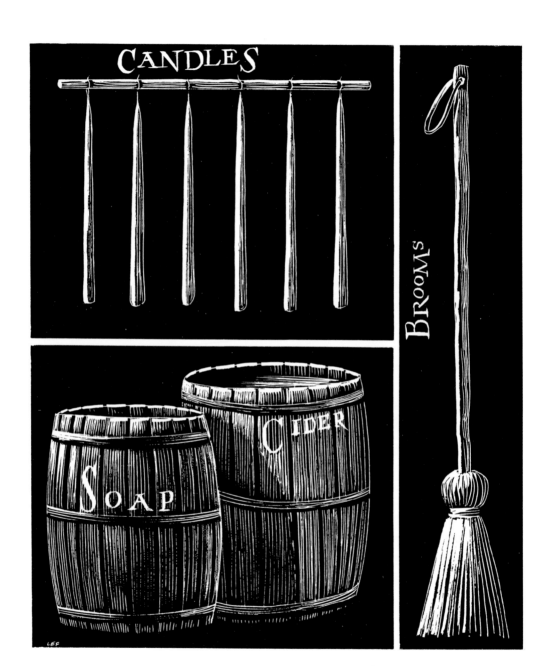

CANDLES

BROOMS

SOAP

CIDER

LEF

COLONIAL CRAFTSMEN

The
HOMEMAKERS

WRITTEN & ILLUSTRATED BY

Leonard Everett Fisher

BENCHMARK BOOKS

MARSHALL CAVENDISH
NEW YORK

Benchmark Books
Marshall Cavendish Corporation
99 White Plains Road
Tarrytown, New York 10591

Library of Congress Cataloging-in-Publication Data
Fisher, Leonard Everett.
The homemakers / written and illustrated by Leonard Everett Fisher.
p.   cm. — (Colonial craftsmen)
Originally published: New York : Franklin Watts, 1973
Includes index.
Summary: Describes how four staples—candles, soap, brooms,
and cider—were made in colonial times.
ISBN 0-7614-0512-7
1. Handicraft—United States—History—Juvenile literature. 2. United States—
History—Colonial period, ca. 1600–1775—Juvenile literature. [1. Home economics.
2. United States—History—Colonial period, ca. 1600–1775.] I. Title.
II. Series: Fisher, Leonard Everett. Colonial craftsmen.
TT23.F56   1998   640.974'09033—dc20   96-38382   CIP   AC

Printed and bound in the United States of America

1   3   5   6   4   2

Other titles in this series

A Brief Introduction

From dawn to dusk, day after day, year after year, most colonial American families had to work endlessly to keep their homes and lives in order.

The countless ordinary household chores necessary for life and survival during the seventeenth and eighteenth centuries, especially in the American wilderness, drove many a settler to early maturity, if not old age. Many men and women reached their thirtieth birthdays having already borne the burden of a lifetime of labor by modern standards.

Families who lived and worked in the more populated port cities of Boston, New York, Philadelphia, or Savannah, had available to them many of the essential goods for running a colonial household. But most of the people who lived outside of the burgeoning commercial urban centers had to make or repair almost everything they needed. These things could have included such items as gloves, straw bonnets, ax handles, nails, and large wooden eating bowls called *trenchards*. Among the most important staple items that could be found in any home — farmhouse or townhouse —were candles, soap, brooms, and cider.

Basic as these things were, it often took more practiced skill to make them than to put them to proper use. More importantly, however, they worked better and seemed to last longer when well made. This was of some concern to the practical-minded colonists who found out soon enough that such everyday articles as commercial candles and soap were either unobtainable or too expensive. Thus many colonists relied on their own skillful hands to make what they themselves needed.

While the simple knowledge and handwork required for many colonial homemaking crafts should not be compared, for example, to the complicated skills and artistry of the silversmith, the same pride of craftsmanship was common to both. And that fundamental attitude — pride in craftsmanship — grew out of the early American necessity to have useful things to ease the toil of life — things which could be depended upon to do the job they were meant to do.

Without craftsmanship, however rustic, there

could be little "product dependability." And "product dependability" was one of the chief elements for survival in the American colonies. It was the same for the hard-working homemaker who manufactured her own candles as it was for the silversmith who fashioned exquisite, gleaming porringers.

Candlemaking

T he chief ingredients for making candles in colonial America were certain coarse animal fats or *tallow* for the waxy part of the candle, and hemp for the wick.

Tallow differed somewhat from other animal body fats in that its basic chemistry was different. It contained a hardening substance which came to be known during the 1800s as *glyceryl stearate* or stearic acid. It was for this chemical reason, although unknown at the time, that tallow was a better fat for candlemaking than grease or other softer body fats. Long after the colonial period, stearic acid was extracted from tallow and then added to it in large concentrations during the commercial manufacturing process of candlemaking.

During most of the colonial period, the best tallow was obtained from sheep or oxen — usually from the leavings of cooked meats that had been saved for a long time. Bear and deer were also sources of tallow. Toward the end of the eighteenth century, some homemakers began to add beeswax and spermaceti — a waxy substance found in the head of a sperm whale — to the melted pure tallow. The addition of these substances tended to increase the hardness of the candles. However, beeswax and spermaceti were so expensive for most homemakers that the practice did not become widespread. Hog tallow was almost never used. Candles made from hog tallow produced choking black smoke, smelled awful, and melted or ran too fast.

In contrast to the crude candles made from hog tallow were those made from the berries of the *candleberry tree* or bayberry bush. Bayberry candles were harder and sturdier than other types of colonial candles. Moreover, they burned more slowly than other candles and were nearly smokeless. But aside from these qualities, the attractive translucent green bayberry candles had an additional characteristic that distinguished them from all others — a pleasant odor, especially after having been extinguished. It was not unusual anywhere in the American colonies to purposely extinguish a burning "bayberry" just to fill a room with its spicy, satisfying aromatic smoke.

The bayberry flourished near the sea and produced silvery-looking berries. These were gathered by colonial children during the autumn months — that time of the year when every colonial household was alive with preparations for the winter ahead, not the least of which was the making of candles. The berries were put into a kettle of boiling water. Their fatty or waxy substance melted and rose to the surface of the boiling water. There it floated, looking like ordinary wax but greenish in color. The "bayberry wax" was then skimmed from the surface and put into another kettle where it was further refined by an additional melting before the actual process of *candledipping* began, or perhaps, *molding*.

The ladies of the colonies used one of three basic methods to make candles: hand-pressing, dipping, or molding.

Hand-pressing required no special knowledge or skill other than extracting wax from beehives. Small bits of warm pliable beeswax were pressed around a hemp wick much as a sculptor does when pushing small chunks of soft clay onto a wire form. The soft wax was then shaped into a crude candle. When the warm and soft pressed candle cooled, it hardened. The hardened wax candle was then ready for use.

The most popular and most painstaking method for making candles in colonial America was dipping.

The work began in and around the great colonial fireplace, the center of so much family activity. There, over a roaring fire and suspended from *trammels,* hooks connected either to *cranes* or to a *backbar*, hung a pair of huge cooking kettles. Cranes were swinging iron bars used to hang pots and other vessels. Because they were hinged, cranes could be swung back and forth, in or out of the blaze, with ease. They came into use sometime after 1700. The backbar, sometimes called a *lugpole*, was a stationary beam built into the top of the fireplace near its front. It served the same purpose as a crane — that is, a bar from which to hang cooking pots. The backbar was not as convenient as a crane since anyone cooking had to reach too close to the fire, if not into it altogether, to remove a hot kettle.

The two great iron kettles hanging from the cranes contained refined tallow. This pure hot

liquid tallow had previously been skimmed from the top of boiling water upon which it had floated. The job of skimming the tallow from the surface of the boiling water was done several times over to obtain the cleanest tallow possible.

In another, cooler area away from the heat of the fireplace, the candlemaker set up two pieces of furniture of equal height, usually two chairs. These were positioned two or three feet apart. Upon the tops of these upright supports, she placed two long poles. And across these poles were laid a series of evenly spaced sticks called *candlerods*. The whole of this equipment looked like a ladder lying horizontally.

Suspended from each candlerod were about a half dozen hemp wicks. The wicks were tightly twisted in a double strand so that they hung from the candlerods by their looped ends.

When the poles and rods with their hanging wicks were ready, and when the melted tallow was just the right temperature — not too hot and certainly not cold — one kettle was dragged over to the dipping area and the slow dipping process was begun. Each candlerod with its six

Rod

Pole

Wicks

or more wicks was carefully dipped into the tallow and returned to its position on the poles. As the kettle being used cooled down, it was replaced with the warmer one still at the fireplace, and put back on the crane for reheating. The two kettles of tallow were thus used alternately as the dipping continued on and on until the desired thickness of the candles was reached.

Each time the candlemaker slowly and carefully dipped a row of wicks for a new coating of tallow, she had to be certain that the tallow in the kettle was not so very hot that it melted off whatever tallow had clung to the wicks in previous dippings. Also, she had to be sure that every dipped row of wicks was cool and hard before the next dipping. If the candles, now growing in thickness with each dip, cooled too fast or were dipped too quickly, they usually cracked or became so brittle that bits and pieces would fall off.

When the candles were finished — that is to say, when the candlemaker decided that her constant dipping had produced, in her opinion, the desired thickness — the loops of the double

twisted wicks encircling the candlerods were snipped. The two remaining ends of each wick were twisted together.

A good worker could dip between 150 and 200 candles in a single day. And there were many skillful candlemaking ladies in the colonies who not only made enough candles for their own family use but enough to supply a lively colonial candle export business to the British West Indies.

Molded candles were made by pouring hot melted tallow into a metal form. These forms or molds were groups of tin cylinders. Large molds might contain from twenty-four to forty-eight candle-shaped cylinders. Regardless of their size, each cylinder contained a wick which hung from a wire stretched across the open top of the mold. When the melted tallow was poured into the cylinder, special care had to be taken to keep the wick straight at all times. This was not especially difficult since the suspended wick was usually drawn through a small opening in the bottom of the mold and pulled taut before the tallow hardened.

Dipped or molded, the new candles were considered too precious to be handled roughly. Usually white in color — unless, of course, they were bayberry green — slender and tapered, newly made colonial candles were carefully packed in special boxes and stored away in some dark corner where sunlight could not discolor them.

Two or three of the candles, however, could always be found in a metal *candelbox* somewhere in the kitchen or near the fireplace where they would be handy and ready for instant use.

Candle Mold

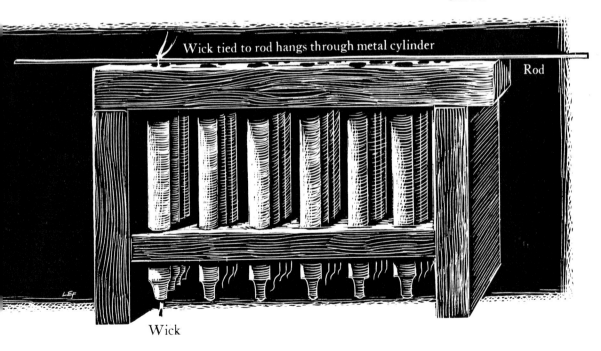

Wick tied to rod hangs through metal cylinder

Rod

Wick

Soapmaking

The eighteenth-century English Methodist minister John Wesley preached "Cleanliness is next to Godliness." Nevertheless, the God-fearing people of colonial America as well as the seventeenth and eighteenth-century people of Western Europe may not have seen it quite this way. In fact, most people, lowborn or highborn, saw little need to wash themselves or the clothes they wore too often.

For the average American, a once-a-month clothes wash was considered ample. Most colonial homemakers let the family wash pile up for two or three months before they did anything about it. In addition, many a colonist washed his body less frequently than he did his clothing. Body-washing baths were considered a health hazard in many places, most especially during the chilling winter months. Bathing one's self with soap and water was avoided like the plague.

Yet, the colonists did wash themselves and their clothing, however infrequently. And they made their own soap to do the job. More accurately, it was usually the young ladies of the family who were given the monotonous task of soapmaking.

Although some hard cakes of soap were produced in early America — and such soap was made with the pleasant-smelling bayberry for personal use — much of colonial soap was a soft, nongreasy, jellylike mass.

The basic method for making soap in colonial America was *leaching*. Leaching is the process of extracting a water-soluble substance from another substance, like ashes, by allowing water to pass through it.

The colonial soapmaker first filled a strongly made tub called a *leach barrel* with wood ashes that had been collected by the bushel during most of the winter and carefully saved. The leach barrel was placed outdoors on a base of either stone, brick, or wood in which had been cut a round groove. Water was then poured into the leach barrel where it filtered down through the ashes until it reached the bottom. As the water filtered down through the ashes, it extracted a substance called *lye*.

A lye solution is a strong liquid cleansing agent that belongs to a family of similar solutions called *alkalines*. Alkalines or alkaline solutions can neutralize acids. Lye by itself is not a soap.

In any event, the lye extracted from the ashes seeped as a solution through the leach barrel into the groove cut into the base upon which the barrel sat. As the drops of lye solution fell or seeped into the groove, they slowly began to flow toward a bucket placed at the end of the groove. Little by little the bucket began to fill.

As the level of ashes in the leach barrel decreased, the soapmaker added more. As she did so, she continued to pour water into the barrel until the bucket at the end of the groove was filled with the lye solution.

The full bucket was then poured into a large iron kettle that hung over an outdoor fire. Previously, the soapmaker had filled the kettle with pounds of cooking grease and animal fat that the colonial family collected all year long. Nothing else was added to these two ingredients. The lye and fat were simply boiled together in the kettle until they combined into a new jellylike substance — colonial soap. The soft soap was stored in a fresh wood barrel ready for use. It took about a day to make enough soap to fill a barrel.

Few colonial homemakers, if any, depended on a precisely written recipe to describe the exact amounts of ash, water, lye, cooking grease, and fat needed to produce soap. They knew by word of mouth and after generations of toil that they could obtain enough lye from five or six bushels of wood ashes. And they knew that when the lye was boiled over an open fire with about twenty to twenty-five pounds of grease and fat, they would end up with a barrel of soft usable soap.

Broommaking

It is not difficult to imagine what a thriving craft broommaking was during the years of colonial settlement.

Dust from summer-dry dirt roads, churned up by breezes, carts, wagons, horsemen, animals, and walkers, floated through every open window, door, and crack in the colonial house. In wet weather it was a somewhat different story. Mud became the culprit — the enemy of every tidy housekeeper. And since the colonial homemaker had no such luxurious device as the modern vacuum cleaner with which to suck up the dirt, dust, and mud that found their way onto every well-pegged floor, there was only the broom to sweep these household foes out the door.

The task of making brooms belonged chiefly to the young men and boys of early America. They were the constant whittlers. They were the energetic and enthusiastic carvers of wood branches who whittled bows and arrows, whistles and wheels, fishing poles, bowls, toys, and what not for pleasure, for profit, and often out of necessity. Plainly, it fell to them to fashion *hemlock* branch brooms and yellow birch splint brooms, sometimes called Indian brooms, with the one valuable tool they all seemed to have owned and treasured — the pocket knife or jack knife.

This is not to say that young girls did not make brooms in the American colonies. Many a farm girl owned a jack knife. And those who did could whittle a broomstick as well as any boy.

The hemlock branch broom was a crude sweeping contraption that required little skill in its manufacture. Simply, an armful of hemlock branches were cut from the tree. Each branch of the hemlock grew smaller shoots which in turn sprouted thousands of small, flat "needles." The branches were tied tightly together at one end with a cord of hemp or some other strong material such as a narrow strip of leather called a thong. Next, the broommaker cut a thick branch from the same tree, whittled or scraped the bark from it, and carved a long sharp point at one end. The pointed end was then jabbed into the tightly bound branches. Once the pointed stick was securely inserted, the broom was finished and ready for immediate use.

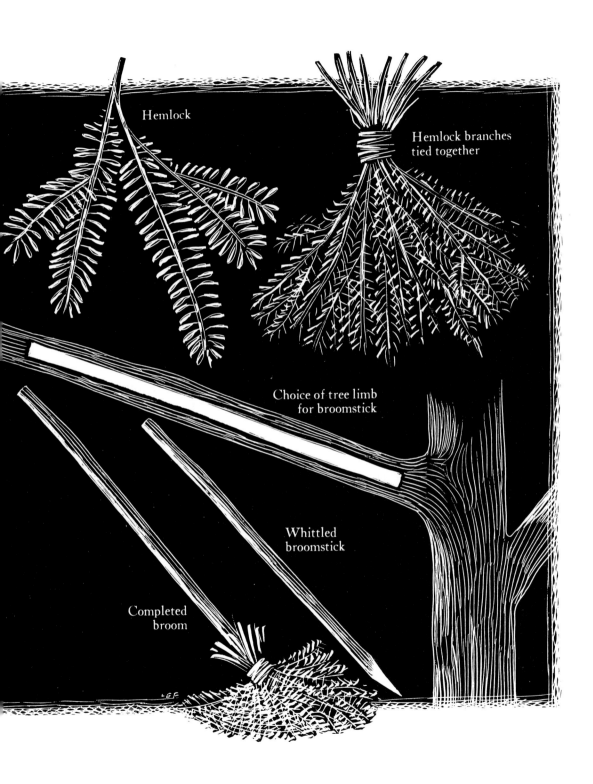

Hemlock

Hemlock branches
tied together

Choice of tree limb
for broomstick

Whittled
broomstick

Completed
broom

The most widely used broom in the American colonies, however, and one more durable than the hemlock branch broom, was the yellow birch splint broom or Indian broom.

This type of broom had its beginnings on the slopes and mountains of northern New England where the yellow birch tree thrived. And there, in New England, the young colonial men and boys not only made enough brooms for their own homes and families, but thousands more for the rest of the American colonies. Sold by itinerant Yankee peddlers, Indian brooms found their way at one time or another into nearly every early American household.

To fashion an Indian "splint" broom, the broommaker first selected a straight, young birch tree — a yellow birch, to be sure — and cut it down. The tree was then trimmed to a six-foot-long stout pole that measured about four or five inches across at its base.

Next, the broommaker cut a two-inch band into the wood approximately twelve to fourteen inches up from the thicker, heavier base. All of the bark below the band was stripped from the

Cut
band

Stripping
bottom
bark

Core

Splintered
bottom
core

tree. With this done, the broommaker, using his sharp jack knife, cut thin, flat strips or slivers — *splints* — from the base upward to the band. He was careful not to detach the splints from the area around the band to which they were connected and from which they now hung freely.

When all of the wood below the band had been completely splintered, that is, sliced into strips, the broommaker stripped the bark from the pole above the band. He then splintered that upper end from the top downward to the band. This time he did not slice away the entire upper portion of the wood as he had done the lower portion. Instead, he left a long wood core that was to become the broomstick.

The upper splinters were then pulled down over the lower splinters. The entire lot was tightly tied together just below the now hidden band and trimmed to the same length at the bottom where they loosely hung.

Finally, the broommaker whittled the stick down to a handy thickness and scraped it smooth either with his jack knife or with a piece of glass. The very last thing he did was to carve a hole through the top of the broomstick to attach a string or leather loop so that the broom could be properly hung.

Core

ipping
top
bark

Splintered
top
core

Untied
drooping
splinters

Tied and
untrimmed
splinters

Completed
and
trimmed
broom

The American colonists drank a variety of liquids. The least of these seemed to be water.

Pale ale, rusty-looking beer, and dark brown porter were drunk in great quantities or *quaffed* almost from the beginning of colonization through the War for Independence. These beverages were all similar, varying only in color and alcoholic content. The chief consumers of beer were the New York Dutch. They wasted little time in constructing breweries wherever they could. Ale was a standard item in almost every New England tavern. Porter could be found most anywhere but seemed to reach the height of popularity in Pennsylvania.

White Madeira and red Port wines were not difficult to buy. Usually, these wines graced the tables of the more worldly aristocrats wherever they lived.

For those who preferred earthy, more intoxicating liquids, there was always rum, a drink distilled from West Indies molasses. Also, rum was liberally mixed with wines, sweet juices, lemons, and limes to make rum *punches*, concoctions that were reserved for festive occasions and served, for the most part, at home.

Metheglin, a strong alcoholic liquor made from honey, was drunk all over the colonies, probably a bit more in Virginia than elsewhere. Fruits, berries, barks, and roots furnished the ingredients for other spirited liquids.

For those who drank no liquor at all or occasionally rested from their alcoholic diets, there was hot chocolate, milk, some coffee — not much at first — Dutch and British tea when the latter was not being boycotted to protest taxation, and peach, pear, and apple juice or *sweet cider*.

Sweet cider was, by far, the cheapest manmade drink in the colonies. Also, it was the most consistently swallowed drink of all.

Made from the pulp of crushed apples, sweet cider was served to children as a substitute for milk or when the family milk supply was low. If the sweet cider was allowed to stand and *ferment* — and it usually was allowed to "age" — its alcoholic content noticeably increased. As the sweet cider aged to become a more alcoholic drink, it was said to have "hardened." Now no longer plain

apple juice, the *hard cider* was ladled out of large barrels, free of charge, to students, parched travelers, thirsty itinerant peddlers, and toiling craftsmen of one kind or another.

The more alcoholic hard cider gradually overtook the average New Englander's thirst for ale. By the time the War for Independence was upon the American colonies, more gallons of hard cider were being consumed than any other beverage.

Cider mills, those sheds and small outbuildings where cider was made, dotted the American countryside wherever apples grew in some abundance. The machinery and process for making colonial cider was not complicated. Bushels of apples were spilled into a homemade bin that contained two or more rollers. The rollers were mounted on simple gears and stood straight up with just a small space between them. The gears were connected to a long arm. The arm, in turn, was hitched to a horse. When the horse moved, the rollers rotated in opposite directions, squashing the apples that fell between.

The mashed apples or *pulp* was scraped from the inside of the bin, from around the rollers, and

Cider Mill

Shaft

Notch

Nut

Cylinders

shoveled into barrels. Sometimes the roller bins were so constructed that the apple pulp fell into a barrel immediately after it had been squashed between the rollers.

However the crushing gadget was constructed, the pulp still had to be squeezed further to extract the drinkable cider. This was done on the *cider press.*

The press was a simple mechanism. At the bottom was a flat wood board or *platform* into which had been cut several channels. These channels converged onto a tin pan or board that hung over a wood bucket. At the top of the press was a large vertical screw from which hung still another flat wood board called a *cover.* The screw was worked by a lever which was inserted into the *screw block* at the proper time.

A layer of straw was placed on the platform upon which was spread the first thick layer of crushed apple, the pulp. Another layer of straw was placed over the pulp and more pulp was added. These alternating layers of straw and crushed apple were continued until the stack was several feet high.

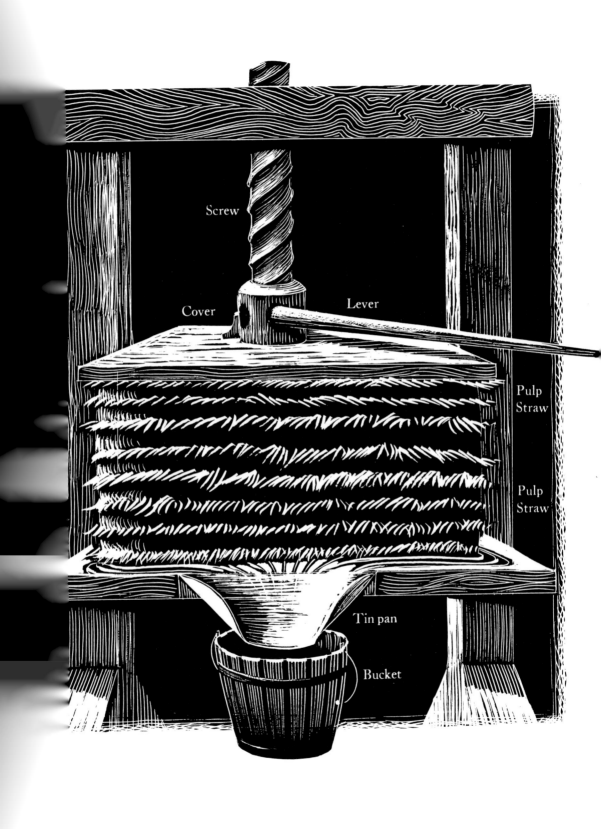

Screw

Cover

Lever

Pulp
Straw

Pulp
Straw

Tin pan

Bucket

Usually, the pulp was absolutely fresh, having been placed on the press just as soon as it was scraped from the bin and rollers. At other times the pulp was allowed to remain in the barrels for a day or so to ferment, become more alcoholic, and in the end produce a harder cider instead of the fresh unfermented sweet cider.

In any event, the lever was placed in the screw block, the screw was turned, and the stack of straw and pulp was squeezed tighter and tighter, smaller and smaller. This pressing action forced the juice to trickle through the straw into the channels and flow out through the pan into the waiting bucket.

When the bucket was full of cider, it was hauled over to a large barrel and dumped as another bucket was placed beneath the pan. And it was from these large barrels that almost every colonial American — man, woman, and child — at some time or other, occasionally or habitually, drank a "goodly" portion of the refreshing, often spirited drink — apple cider.

LEONARD EVERETT FISHER is a well-known author-artist whose books include *Alphabet Art, The Great Wall of China, The Tower of London, Marie Curie, Jason and the Golden Fleece, The Olympians, The ABC Exhibit, Sailboat Lost,* and many others.

Often honored for his contribution to children's literature, Mr. Fisher was the recipient of the 1989 Nonfiction Award presented by the *Washington Post* and the Children's Book Guild of Washington for the body of an author's work. In 1991, he received both the Catholic Library Association's Regina Medal and the University of Minnesota's Kerlan Award for the entire body of his work. Leonard Everett Fisher lives in Westport, Connecticut.